507

C708 019 637 426 B2

C000255927

JOHN REDM   and worked in
Oxford, Liver   edits the literary
magazine *Gall*   for the *Guardian*,
t   and the *LRB*. His poetry collection *Thumb's Width* was
           by Carcanet Press in 2001, and his *How to Write a Poem* by
         in 2005. John Redmond teaches Creative Writing at the
      y of Liverpool.

Also by John Redmond from Carcanet Press

Thumb's Width

JOHN REDMOND

MUDe

CARCANET

Nottinghamshire County Council Community Services	
821. 92 RED	
Askews	
	£9.95

First published in Great Britain in 2008 by
Carcanet Press Limited
Alliance House
Cross Street
Manchester M2 7AQ

Copyright © John Redmond 2008

Quotations from Robert D. Putnam, *Bowling Alone*, reprinted with the
permission of Simon and Schuster Adult Publishing Group and the author.
Copyright © 2000 by Robert D. Putnam. Quotations from Régis Debray,
God: An Itinerary, included by permission of Verso.

The right of John Redmond to be identified as the author of this work
has been asserted by him in accordance with the
Copyright, Designs and Patents Act of 1988
All rights reserved

A CIP catalogue record for this book is available from the British Library
ISBN 978 1 85754 927 0

The publisher acknowledges financial assistance from Arts Council England

Typset in Bembo by XL Publishing Services, Tiverton
Printed and bound in England by SRP Ltd, Exeter

To my brother

Acknowledgements

I would like to thank the editors of the following publications in which some of these poems appeared: the *Irish Times*, *Thumbscrew*, *Metre*, *In the Red*, *PN Review*, *Poetry Wales* and *The Recorder*.

'Grand Theft America' was published by the Liverpool University Centre for Poetry and Science (www.poetryandscience.co.uk). 'MUDe', Part 2, was published by *New Welsh Review*. 'Frisk' was published in a limited edition of 50 copies by Treganna Press, Cardiff, in collaboration with the artist Alun Hemming.

Contents

Part 1

Suburbanization of the last thirty years has increased not only our financial investment in the automobile, but also our investment of time. Between 1969 and 1995, according to government surveys of vehicle usage, the length of the average trip to work increased by 26 percent, while the average shopping trip increased by 29 percent. While the number of commuting trips per household rose 24 percent over this quarter century, the number of shopping trips per household almost doubled. And each trip was more likely to be made alone ...

Robert D. Putnam, *Bowling Alone:*
The Collapse and Revival of American Community
(New York: Simon and Schuster, 2000)

The *autoyen*, the car-driving citizen, is a drifter, a shirker of civic responsibility, and a notorious abstentionist (civic space being pedestrian and walkable, on the model of the Greek *polis*). He is haunted by an indifference to place, a spirituality of escapism, and a constantly hurried faith. He is no longer the walker along side roads .... He chooses his points of anchorage, makes his groupings an expression of his will.

Régis Debray, *God: An Itinerary*
(London and New York: Verso, 2004)

The Clown Lounge

From the Clown Lounge to the Mall of America with love and kisses
– 'Can you pass the CD? It's under your seat' –
From the sole copy of *Fargo* in stock – 'Context?' –
to the SUVs parked on the lake – 'I *cannot*
believe she drives one.' – From wearing
shorts all winter to swallowing bongwater, from walk-in
wardrobes to Kofi on the webpage
from emo-rock and rent-a-wreck
to monster-trucks and ostrich-on-
a-stick – 'There are seats at
the front. You should just come in.' –
From Greg's driving – 'I never *hit*
anything' – to Nick's capture
of a traffic-cone without stopping – 'Don't drive
like my brother!' – From the dead bat
on the department floor – 'Watch out!
It could give you rabies!' – to student
response-sheets – 'Don't set
Self-Portrait in a Convex Mirror again – it
is bad.' – From barmen who wear hats
– 'Unless you don't want to come in ...' –
to the goths and gamers sitting furthest from the door
– 'Hi! Welcome to our conversation!' –
From the pillar of fire
above an Indian casino – 'Do you
want to come in?' – to the roadsign
approaching Lake George: 'BUMP↓' From 'Operation
Enduring Imperialism' – 'I thought
it would be a small Chicago...' –
to the soccer moms in outer-ring suburbs
– 'but it isn't.' – From not getting the Stone
Roses to not getting Ted Hughes
– 'he's too straight for me' – from the wrong
side of the car – 'I'm sorry' –
to the logging-towns which cut down northern Minnesota
– 'and they're *proud* of it!' – from never meeting
a fratboy – 'That works' –

to never meeting a Republican
– 'You should vote for my Dad.
He has a good heart.' –
From the secret highway exit for St. Paul
– 'Did I apologise for my driving?' –
to 'the best liberal arts college in urban Minnesota.'
From Jessica Lange's cheekbones
– 'Could some of your posters not be
of white male writers?' – to a quiet tradition
of streakers. From the katydids
that Forrest brought to class
– 'True visionaries don't know the meaning of "no"!' –
to that slow lunar
smudge above the Clown Lounge
– 'Time to dust the sky for fingerprints.' – From me
to you, Mac, with hugs and kisses
– 'You should totally come in. Come in' –
and don't drive like *his* brother.

Bemidji

The last American of the season
has collapsed through the ice.

The ice-fishing village has gone.
The lake hovers out of winter
with its last ice-fishing house,
empty as an afterlife with one refrigerator.

It could be yours … this life, that SUV …
to scrape across a sunlit outer space,
before the Mississippi weakens,

with the yet-to-be-caught swerving beneath you,
with all the rusting of the yet-to-be-retrieved.

Bemidji – 'where the water crosses' –
the Ojibwa word for the lake
upholds a lakeside town
as it whitens, each year, with discovery.

You would drive out there with windows down
to open your door in the pressure.

Stoltz

They crash, we hear
two parts – braking –

bodywork. We
turn but it is over.
They climb out, swap
details and separate –

with the speed
they turned into each other
now in turning away.

Their half-wrecks face the corner-shops –
Stoltz (the laundry, this side),

Breadsmith (the bakery, opposite)
where faces (like ourselves) face
south, south, down, southwest,

then all west as the law arrives.

The SUV went east into the small car turning south –
(*due* east and *due* south –
because the roads are built for the sun).

I was facing the wrong direction.

St. Paul?

St. Paul, what can I
say? In a way that
says it all ... I look
for your pavements (so
expertly kept)
under my bootsoles.
Swift after snowfall
your householders' brushes
appeared to swish
all death-traps away
(yet one house with
Wiccan symbols
strove to be 'odd' –
'odd' as in 'an exception'.)
I think of you too as
'swept back' somehow,
like my landlord's
fretful office-lady,
holding yourself in
with a permanent Alice
band, saying *should*
with the startled
eyebrows of a facelift.
And as for religion ...
On the road to St. Cloud,
your heavenly-sounding
neighbour I would
never actually see,
I read the 'Adopt
a highway' signs as
all there was to read.
So much for conversion.
At night, leaving work
(the one place I had
to walk) not a soul
would be abroad,
meanwhile your houses –

rich and graciously lit –
crashed together like
regular ice-cubes.
That your police shut
parties down, that
my snowball-throwing
students had to flee –
being 'underage' –
that no one was poor
(though everyone was needy)
these, too, say it all.
'Would you like a cat?'
(a mood so you:
neither interrogative
nor imperative, but
both at once). 'We
won't be angry if
you say no ...
but we will be sad.'

Everything worked.
So everyone did.

Double Felix

Her fur is for
portraiture.

His purr is far
more appreciative.

Rough comparison
effects a pair –

togetherness
as of two paws –

though, side by side,
the compared stare

apart, their pursuits
separate: sloth

(hers); ladybugs,
dust and her (his).

All night he pursues
her – but for fun,

nothing further.

Grand Theft America

Though upside-down, my burning stickshift
    leapfrogs Chinatown – 'Hey!
Learn how to drive!' – though crashed to bits,
    my crumbling Hummer
outguns the runaway underground train,
    and though bumpy men
with baseball-bats rebuff my tiny life
    – 'Take him out!' – I
will make a junction to pinch a jalopy – 'Suspect
    thinks he can play
fast and loose with the law' – with a flick
    of the pinkie, switch
from first- to third- to first-person view
– 'You know something? I *am* hot tonight' –
    full-on front-end
a hatchback and thrill (with a slo-mo jump
    across the rush-hour)
to the dark and light of police helicopters
    blowing apart
in bootsole view. And I will wait till the kettle
    pulls itself
off ('You see? The passion,
she is back'), let my left hand drift to my left cheek,
    park myself deep
in the alleyway murk (press middle finger to exit)
    and twitch,
or go round and round
    and twitch.
And I will let my right hand explore my chin-jut
    till sundown, and I will check
out the arc of my shotgun (mmmm how good
    this tastes),
as America loads in the background.

Limo

You wouldn't want this front-seat in your face
if you were me, if I were you,
so much in-your-face the Manhattan view
is cut and carved like a crust
about its bulbous sheen. You wouldn't want to guess
how much of life goes over my head
and yours – flyover by flyover – in thin slices
of distance around the driver's head:
small dreams where you wouldn't want
to live. For if you were he, and I
were you, we wouldn't pause here as he
must, where the pot-bellied bridges reflect
reflections from the road. We would make a fist also
and have it, as the streetsign does,
that says, *Our Lady of Snows.*

Futon

Not to be hard on
my no longer
horizontal nor,
in truth, indispensable
futon, it must
weigh a ton and barely
nudges out of
a room it was not
so hard to be in –
a half-contribution
to my half-employed
English majors (God
bless them) one of whom
holds up the other end.
Over my shoulder
the flat is emptying –
dust of a time
I haven't had time
to erase. And this –
the sole expensive
item, the vanishing
skeleton of my nights,
we wobble and wrestle
down the stairwell

to Nick's decrepit
Lincoln. On his less
than kingsize roof
he lashes it calmly
after a fashion
to mirrors, to bumpers,
with enterprising
improbable twine,
and it feels so light,
as he drives off,

to be on foot.

JFK to LGA

Sliding doors, driven again,
(one airport to another)
the low driverless sun
gets in, gets over everyone,
patterns us front and side,
makes us slit and turn
red undefended eyes,
the out-of-focus shuttle-
passengers and I, swaying
as a man from bend to bend,
from shoulder to hard shoulder,
gathered here together,
amidst the illuminated
snot-trails of the windscreen
reflecting on each other.

Omey

Oh my. Sunk wheels, low tide –
my aunts in a spin. Soft sand

has sucked – no, suckered – us in
and I'm not saying who's to blame –
am I?
        Omey Island. Almost Mayo.
We aimed to see the midden here,

the skulls in the surface coming up for air,
which still remain to be seen as we …
Reverse! Now try! Try now! Reverse!

What we wouldn't give for four-wheel drive.

As mother plots to dig us out
before the ocean divvies us up,

I spot across the grey horseracing space
the ominous makings of help:

male figures. They wave,
                I watch
and I wonder why I mind so much
that we won't be found in the morning.

Frisk

When he ambled out of the world and shut
the door, I wonder what my father found,
with a swift nervy frisk, was left behind?
'I am a fool!' He'd say this aloud,
the way I do sometimes, leaving the flat,
turning back for some necessary trash,
opening the door as he is coming out.

Gliomach

Over the inver the universe blows –
father dives into the hereafter

('Where?' 'Here!')
the vanishing point of authoritative shoulders.

Stars wend,
('What?') heavens weave

between wide-angled jungles of seaweed
as he pours in ('Here!')
upside-down,
a slow flow of reflections from his mouth:

'is fánach an áit a bhfaighfeá gliomach'

smoking us out in Irish
one more time ('Where is *here?*')
pulling back evergreen waves of structure –

'it's a queer place you would find a lobster'.

Part 2

The archetypal interaction with a new pal on the Internet lacks precisely the social embeddedness that seems essential to overcome the lack of social cues within the medium itself. Face-to-face networks tend to be dense and bounded, whereas computer-mediated communication tends to be sparse and unbounded. Anonymity and fluidity in the virtual world encourage 'easy in, easy out,' 'drive-by' relationships.

Robert D. Putnam, *Bowling Alone:*
The Collapse and Revival of American Community
(New York: Simon and Schuster, 2000)

Our new information and communication technologies unsettle simultaneously the mode of reproduction of texts, their support, and our ways of reading. With the dematerialized (and, into the bargain, desacralized) book begins an a-biblical world, invaded by 'culture' and deserted by the practice of reading. *A-biblical* may be said of a world in which writing circulates more cheerfully than it did before, but in which the book, transformed into a database manipulable at will, has lost its symbolic centrality, which now accrues to utilitarian printouts and selective reappropriations. The book in fragments. God in pieces?

Régis Debray, *God: An Itinerary*
(London and New York: Verso, 2004)

MUDe

*I lost a few goddesses on my way from south to north,
as well as many gods on my way from east to west.*

Szymborska

First Session

As you move, you turn living again.
>east
No such exit
>west
No such exit
>listen
Nothing to speak of.
>look
A dark room.
You feel a slight draught.
A small voice intones: When demons climb the dandelions ...
Hands are pressing you down.
#Girouette: anyone want to party?
You find it hard to breathe.
A small voice intones: When goblins spread the heather ...
>look at hands
It is too dark to look at hands.
#Doodelsack: sure, if u tank ...
A small voice intones: When dells are dark with tiny hands ...
You are suffocating.
You twist and thrash for air!
#Girouette: fine xroads in 2?
>up
You mouth for air but no air comes!
Hands are pressing you down.
A small voice intones: Deep in the ground is better!
You sink downwards!

                    crosshatched bewitchery
        distributed

        wisp to wisp

with a swish
          of slow hooked crashes

the crispest
of crisp blades insist

 on their rich persistent struggle

                    this
          rough indoor drizzle

>out
You grasp a hand and wrestle bravely!
*Cuckoospell shouts: The jig is up! *leaps out of the window**

You feel a large weight off your shoulders.

>look
Shredded darkness. A barn. The hay spreads out in every direction,
a tremendous disorder of humps and hollows. When you walk, the
surface twitches and your legs vanish below the knee. Although the
walls are not easy to make out, you can tell from the pitch of the
roof this once was a house. To the south a small window, half-lost
in all the confusion, gleams up densely.
  The only obvious exit is west.
  Your ten-year-old self is here.
Your ten-year-old self exclaims: Thou shalt not twist my fingers,
  mortal one!
*Awf shouts: Stop him! Stop him! Somebody stop that orc! *runs into the
broom-closet**
You feel a slight draught
#Doodelsack thinks about a bashing unique and drools copiously
Your ten-year-old self explodes a hay-shower in your face – seeds
  and wisps splatter your nose and mouth.
#Girouette: skills? align?

You have a tremendous urge to sneeze.

#Doodelsack adjusts his halo, adopts a prayerful pose, and murmurs sweetly: my polearm is 82 – and rising.

Your ten-year-old self wipes the sweaty hair from his eyes.

*Momworship shouts: *runs about with arms outstretched* don't worry Cuck I gotcha! I gotcha!*

SCHNUGHZZ! You send the contents of your nose glittering around the room.

*Cuckoospell shouts: erm, on second thoughts *puts on the brakes in mid-air**

Your ten-year-old self imitates you: Schnucks!

>throw hay at boy

You gather an armful of hay and hurl it at boy!

Your ten-year-old self shakes the debris from his hair and blows a wisp from his mouth

Your ten-year-old self climbs an unsteady mound of hay

*Momworship shouts: *pout**

>tackle boy

You attempt to tackle small boy but your timing is off!

You fall flat on your face!

Your ten-year-old self somersaults on top of you!

You sink downwards!

       an impenetrable script of equivalence
thus a structure occurs

      here

     coarse as
orc-hair
      much-preoccupied tresses

      stress and thatch
these rife insurrectionary chutes

     that ease to unstretch

    from stitch to stitch

Your ten-year-old self spins and bounces on the hay.

Your ten-year-old self scrambles west.
>west
Your feet depress the surface with outlandish strides.
The ruin of a house that serves as a barn. You are high – near the rafters – on a minor plateau of hay which thickens the darkness with musk and heat. The fuzzy lumps of gloom lighten westward where the hay drops abruptly to the floor of the barn. The top of a ladder emerges conveniently from the tangle.

   Obvious directions: east, down
Girouette shouts: Would owner of sacred poleaxe please send me a tell?
>down
You take a creaky grip on the ladder and clamber to the floor.
The floor of the barn is covered in debris: dust, seeds, wisps, little beards of straw. To the north, the entrance – a large rectangle of daylight – leans an ambivalent shoulder against the darkening banks of hay. To the west, a dilapidated wall has internalised – how queer – the shape of a fireplace, and a doorway leads to a small back-room. Elsewhere the hay rises sharply, so that it feels like you are in a hallway and, to the east, the feet of a ladder peek out.

   Obvious directions: north, west, ladder.

   Your ten-year-old self is here.

   Godsend the utter novice is here
Aunt Kate walks in.
Godsend exclaims: Help!
Your ten-year-old self showers you with chaff
Aunt Kate scoops salt from a bucket and scatters it backhanded over the hay.
Godsend asks: How do you kill things?
Your ten-year-old self sticks out his tongue.
>shrug Godsend
You shrug helplessly at Godsend
Aunt Kate says: Easy there now, fellow-me-lad, none of your jumping around.
Your ten-year-old self adopts the voice of Aunt Kate: I was born in a barn! I was born in a barn and it did me no harm!
Your ten-year-old self leaves north
#Godsend: Can anyone here tell me how to kill things?
Aunt Kate says: I don't know … wouldn't he wear you out?
Aunt Kate looks at you, brings two fingers to her mouth, and raises her eyebrows to suggest a cigarette.

>nod
You nod solemnly
Aunt Kate leaves north
#Puerice: ★sigh★ with difficulty, Godsend, with difficulty ...
>north
Your skin feels damp in the breeze.
The outskirts of a barn. From the north a lane sweeps down, higgledy-piggledy, curving its great middlethatch of grass between low stone walls towards the sea. It splits in two and vanishes: east to a whitewashed house, and west to a gated field. Loose clumps of hay bestrew the many footsteps, hoofmarks and wheelruts. To the southeast, lies the shore. To the south, the barn's dark entrance.
  Obvious directions: east, west, north, south, southeast.
  Aunt Kate is here
  Mother is here
  Your ten-year-old self is here
  Some damp clumps of hay are here (drying in the sun)
Your ten-year-old self collects a large wedge of hay so that only his legs are visible and disappears into the barn.
Mother twists her fingers together in an agitated fashion
Aunt Kate lights her cigarette and takes a deep drag.
Mother asks: Have any of you seen him? I've called and called ...
Aunt Kate shakes her head and says: Is he off again, the unfortunate creature?
#Godsend flexes his muscles, bursting his greaves and bracers: TELL ME HOW TO KILL THINGS!
A full haywain rattles down the lane drawn by a confused-looking donkey.
Godsend arrives.
Mother exclaims: What has happened? Oh, what has happened?
#Fanboy: Godsend, a hot tip: type: suicide <password>
The donkey rattles the haywain to a stop and tries to make out that nothing has happened.
Your ten-year-old self arrives, throwing a bunch of hayseed over Mother
#Filthypiglet: Well, you could enter the Dark Tower and demand to see the management ...
Mother snaps: Would you leave off your fooling, you little brat, and help me find your father!
Your ten-year-old self bows his head.

#Sulphur says, 'Try this', snapping his fingers. A squirrel explodes in the forest.

Mother exclaims: Will nobody help me?

Godsend asks: How do you kill things?

#Fanboy says, 'Try this', leaping from his steed at the last moment. The posse sweeps over the cliff

Mother wails

Mother leaves southeast

Aunt Kate takes a deep drag and blows out some nice circles

A Fire Spirit arrives

An Orc tithe-collector arrives

Spirit cracks a fire-whip above its head. Light flows in many directions.

Aunt Kate shivers with fear

Donkey pulls a haywain east

The heat and light from the Spirit cause you to avert your face.

Godsend asks: Hey, should we fight these guys?

>shake

You shake your head

#Oompah: Someone here in the building is about to get fired or terribly reprimanded.

Orc snivels: In the emperor's name! Twenty gold coins!

A gleam of resentment burns briefly in Aunt Kate's eyes

Godsend exclaims: Aw, come on we can take them!

Godsend kicks Orc

>ack

You ack

Orc snivels: Death to the sneaky humans! Death! Death!

Spirit's mouth glows: I HEAR AND OBEY, MASTER

#Oompah: Because my boss just came in and had me help him spell 'insubordinate'.

Spirit sucks a ball of flame from its right shoulder and hurls it clock-wise into the barn.

The barn goes up in orange and black.

Aunt Kate pulls a small boy away east

Godsend exclaims: Oops!

Godsend leaves north

Spirit slashes your leg with a flaming sword, blood flies in many directions.

#Fanboy falls off his Nazgul laughing.

You swing and miss.

It looks as if rain might be on the way.

Spirit gurgles: MUHAHAHA

#Cuckoospell: *ponder* Perhaps it was a warning?

>south

A burning barn. The hay churns with lethal heat. As the suddenly visible walls blister with self-understanding, a scorched ladder floats into the inferno. The entrance to the north is blindingly white.

  Obvious directions: north, west, ladder

Spirit blazes in

Spirit crushes your arm with a scorching maul, blood flies in many directions.

You swing and miss

#Oompah: Well 'warning' fits under 'terribly reprimanded'.

>west

The back-room of a barn. In outline, a few scattered implements – an old pitchfork, a rake, a bucket, the wheel of an overturned barrow. Smoke funnels lugubriously, in blue-grey waves, towards a little window.

  The only obvious exit is east

You feel a slight draught

Spirit blazes in

Spirit smashes your chest with a blazing hammer, blood flies in many directions.

You land a light blow on Spirit's foot.

Spirit throws back his head and cackles with glee!

#Cuckoospell: TO YOU. Perhaps it was a warning to you

>climb out window

You scramble out the window and land awkwardly on the shore.

The tide is almost half-way in. Dry weed crinkles beneath your step. Here and there, amidst the collaborative sheen of pebble and shell, a few large rockpools please your eye. To the north, you see the pockmarked rear of a barn.

  Obvious directions: east, west.

  Father is here

  Mother is here

Father strides into the water swiping at it with his sword

Father exclaims: We have unfinished business, you and I!

Mother tries in vain to pull Father back

Mother exclaims: Leave off, will you, please! For my sake!

Spirit blazes in

#Oompah scratches his head until a lightbulb appears.

Spirit pierces your neck with a white-hot lance, blood flies in many directions.

You die.

You notice a tear in the fabric of reality.

It starts very far up, it goes very far down and splits you precisely in half.

The tear gets wider as Death's craggy knuckles struggle in.

He is opening you methodically like an egg.

#The Guildmaster, his heart in flames, records the passing of Ferdia from the Material Plane.

#Weaselfish acks

#Fanboy acks.

#Lurkio doubles over and pukes

#Tundrapanic goes white and faints.

#Zigzag sits in dark thought on the rainy stair.

Your grainy contents explode into the tear.

#Oompah acks.

There is no size. There never has been.

Death pushes a whole finger through.

His finished hand is at once all sizes there ever have been, all sizes there ever will be, all sizes there ever could be.

Death's finger is the size of Death's arm is the size of your finger is the size of your arm is the size of you

#Auf goes stiff in the saddle and falls off his horse.

#Chosenhelm lays the body of Ferdia on a makeshift skiff. He covers the body with much-beloved things then steps back solemnly. He touches a burning brand to the skiff and sets it adrift on dark-reflecting waters.

Death's eye looks fixedly out of the meal he has made of you.

Your mouth is forced open as wide as it can go. Then wider. Death tumbles inside with his six wet arms.

#Bedequiver puts down his drink, beer flowing magnificently from his chin. He looks from face to face around the bar, murdering a slow, elfin keen in Ferdia's memory.

He starts to swallow your throat from the inside. He starts to swallow you and your throat.

With his six strong arms, Death clings to the surface of your soul like a small black lizard.

He chews happily in time with the endless bobbing of blue cosmic waves.

#Cuckoospell sees the deeds of Ferdia written out in soft white letters which meander – gently – to the stars.

His reptilian face keeps changing. It is trying on all the expressions you have ever worn and ever will have worn.

His smile is a crack within a crack.

He is chewing things over.

He begins to look mildly disappointed.

He runs through all the mildly disappointed faces you have ever attempted.

Finally, he shakes the shapelessness of his head and laughs.

'You know, Mortal One, you really *can't* get good soul these days.'

Death brings up everything he has swallowed.

Above the shiny black tumult, he spits you out very high.

And very very far.

As if there truly were a thing called size.

You splatter against a stone wall and stick.

Then you start rolling down.

#Jackfrost stares grimly from the summit.

Your surroundings seem familiar.

The Church of St Kieran.

A big rabbit wineskin of pina colada (almost empty).

A small white card.

Some tights.

A sprig of St John's Wort.

A large bulletin board mounted on the wall.

Uberscram the Chevalier is here.

Some mist is here.

Sleeveen the Sneak is lying here (dead)

Tundrapanic the Missionary is writing a message here.

The village watchman is here ensuring domestic tranquility.
The watchman glows with a bright light!
   Obvious directions: north, south.
#Lurkio's magic carpet is almost holed by the star of Ferdia rising
>pray
You roll to the bottom of the wall and reappear in material form.
Some mist leaves south.
>get sprig
You get the St John's Wort
#Zigzag pats his pockets for a reality pill
>heal wounds
You carefully apply St John's Wort to your wounds
#Beesmoke stops at the end of the balcony, murmuring to herself:
   Folded in time is that sailing day,
   through the rapt distresses of a waterfall: a sky
   with a face too big to take in at once;
   a sea of faces which took us in completely
   and our being taken in by an island of delph
   and chivalry and shiny, haphazard shelves
   which repeatedly drifted like the self
   into a pattern of contemplation:
   a dolphin with a look of almost elfin satisfaction.

Second Session

#*Steerpike leaps from his coffin. It is time!*
>look
The harbour tavern. Slow-moving, murky customers. Most of the
light and all of the smoke weave south from a vast fireplace. Various
salvaged items – barrels, chests, beams, even an impressive anchor
on the wall – lend the room the look of a shipwreck. The landlord,
a ravaged dwarf, leans across a low, dark-stained counter – on which
his menu is the darkest stain of all.
   The only obvious exit is east.
   Oompah the limestone formation is here
   Awf the lord of the woods is here
   Sulphur and Twitch are playing cards here
>drink blood
You chug down some Hobbit Blood and feel refreshed!
Swivel falls in from the cold
The barman clears his throat: The newest of food, the oldest of
   drink!
You wipe the blood from your chin in satisfied fashion.
#*Steerpike glances around. Mayhap he is too early?*
Twitch asks: Should we throw another peasant on the fire?
Father arrives.
Sulphur spits in the grate. A conflagration blazes up.
Father walks to the counter, frisks his pockets and pulls them out –
   white and empty.
Oompah rolls east.
Father looks at you embarrassed.
Twitch washes down a worm with Dragon's Spit
Father looks at you embarrassed.
Father looks at you embarrassed.
>nod barman
You nod solemnly to the barman
The landlord shoots you a knowing smile. He takes five of your
   gold coins and pours out a drink for Father.
Father takes the drink, mildly rolls his eyes, and invites you to join
   him on a nearby barrel.
#*Steerpike crawls back into his coffin to have a cigarette.*
>sit

You pull up a barrel and sit down awkwardly.

Father takes a deep gulp of his pint and regards you slowly. His
  gloomy eyes protrude.

You burp.

Father smiles wanly. He tips his glass so that a small pool of Hobbit
  Blood forms on the table.

The pool starts to dribble towards the table's western edge.

Swivel finds the darkest corner of the tavern, draws in his cloak,
  and hangs from the rafters.

Father regards the pool and studies its undulation over the rough
  surface. He meditates for a while, slowly shaking his head.

The pool draws closer to the edge of the table.

Father draws his dagger. His eyes shine queerly in the firelight.

Twitch looks up from his playing-cards.

Father sinks his dagger into the pool. He stabs it deliberately with
  short quick strokes!

The pool rolls to the table's edge where it collects in a glittering
  bulge.

Father sits back in melancholy fashion.

>examine table

A shape has been stabbed into the surface of the table.

#Steerpike surveys his coffin. All he can see is one red eye.

>examine shape

It looks like a child has drawn a house in blood.

The pool rolls over the edge.

Third Session

#Odile: *Did you ever see anything like the rain?*

#Godsend: *YOU ARE ALL A BUNCH OF LOSERS!*

#Gubbertusk: *You weren't talking about me, were you?*

#Twitch *lowers his visor*

#Njar *swerves off the road*

Dudesong *shouts: OK Eurotrash, out front right now! *cracks knuckles together**

#Tundrapanic: *Is there a way to throw someone out of the Eldar?*

Father looks at you with large watery eyes

#Godsend: *U SHOULD KNOW DUMBASS YOU JOINED IT*

#Zigzag: *Sometimes when I get down on my knees*
and her feet are deeply armed ...

Odile *rests her right stiletto on Zigzag's throat*

The barman shouts: The newest of food, the oldest of drink!

#Gubbertusk: *where do u get off calling everyone a dumbass?*

#Zigzag: *by the unconstricted blackness of her heels*
when the sky is making
inroads through a window or a door ...

#Sulphur *dives out of the sun: We gave you goons the Statue of Liberty,*
now we're taking it back!

Father unsheathes his dagger

#Manshape *dives down a rabbit-hole*

Father asks: Will you join me in this, captain?

#Lurkio *enters an oak-hollow.*
Surely no one will follow ...

#Oompah *carefully unscrews Godsend's fingers from the caps lock*

#Zigzag: *a momentary light*
scrolls down a polished leather curve,
slimming as it extends, ...

You hear a loud banging on the roof

Father leaves east

#Gubbertusk: *how old are you anyway?*

>east

The village harbour. Lightning veins the sky. As you fight against the rainstorm, the fishing-cage shadows criss and cross in numerous directions. A road leads north into the village. A little tavern gleams to the west.

Obvious directions: south, west, north
  Father is here.
#*Zigzag: as though a button unwound*
              to the width of a hair-
              and as my eyelashes broach the surface ...
#*Njar is crushed by a falling Volkswagen*
#*Godsend: WHATS IT TO U TUSKFUCK*
#*Beesmoke passes the bong*
#*Zigzag: this enchanted keyhole melts before me,*
              through which I spy a house, compressed
              and intricately finned, ...
You struggle forward against the flowing sheets of rain
#*Tundrapanic: I say we go after this twerp*
#*Mumchance leads the shadow host across the ocean floor*
#*Doodelsack opens his bloodshot eyes to music from the Twilight Zone*
#*Zigzag: like a candle-flame*
              over a vertical, black-veined sea ...
#*Gubbertusk: You'd get banished if we killed him*
Father shakes his fist at the storm
#*Tundrapanic: dude I have alts*
#*Odile betrays the makings of a smile to Zigzag*
#*Tundrapanic: He won't know who they are either ;)*
#*Cuckoospell lifts the Staff of Silence towards America. Jukeboxes fail from*
  coast to coast.
#*Auf grabs a white flag, pulls on his Bono-mask, and swings through the*
  rainforest
#*Oompah: A five-hour session while my boss thinks I'm working furiously.*
  Man, this rules!
Father raises his dagger high and charges down the pier
#*Zigzag: and, on that flame's reflection,*
              two ghostly dots
              striving, as like as not,
              against the half-lit abducting tide ...
#*Odile: wanna get married upstairs in the rain?*
#*Godsend: just think you kill me you get banished well whats that mean to*
  me NOT A DAMN THING I hope your dumb prolly white ass gets
  kicked off this damn game for life cos you suck major fucking dick
The sea flexes into a tremendous overhanging wave.
#*Godsend: BITE MY FAT ASS IM GONE*
#*Zigzag: Then she lifts her foot to the next stair,*
              bright with the reflection of what is not there.

Fourth Session

>east

A tumbledown room. A table against the northern wall thoroughly sprayed with roof-chaff. In the southwest corner a ramshackle chair. Against the western wall, the damp black corpse of a bed, its springs bent in many directions.

  A solitary window admits soft light.

  The only obvious exit is west.

>look out window

You make out the edge of the sea-wall, a mild definition from which the low tide wheels into twilight. The underlit waves look wan and jittery. A blustery, shower-laden wind distresses the water, causing arcs to form in several directions.

#Cuckoospell *watches a ribbon of outer space*
  rise like smoke from the sleepy hamlet

You feel a slight draught.

>examine bed

The rusty old springs twist blackly towards your face. The bed's centre has declined to bursts of rubbish on the floor.

You ponder the identity of the last occupant.

A big drop of water stretches from the ceiling.

>search room

Something drifts west across the floor, falls violently between the cracks.

>west

A murky hallway. Doorways, which have no doors, lead east and west while a staircase, with barely half its stairs, surmounts the gloom. Between the treacherous floor-cracks, fragments of slate form melancholy clusters. A dirty, spotted mirror hangs on the western wall.

  Obvious directions: east, west, up.

>examine mirror

As you pass close, a darkness gusts to its surface.

#Beesmoke *starts a ribbon of silence*
  spiralling from her Hamlet cigar

A little ball bounces in

>examine ball
You notice it has a faint red glow.
The ball stops at your feet.

A big drop of water strikes you on the face!

>get ball
Before you can touch the ball, it rolls away west.
#Smirch conjures a puff of Beesmoke
with a slithery rub of his storm-lamp
You think you can hear a seagull crying.
>west
Nettles rise and fall over what is left of the house's kitchen area.
While the walls, to the south and north, are badly fractured, the
western wall has completely disappeared – in its absence you admire
the bay sweeping under broken steelblue clouds towards sundown.
The only intact wall is east, where an old fireplace nests out of the
wind.
  Obvious directions: east, west, south.
  Your ten-year-old self is here
  A little ball is here
#Beesmoke flows up in the blue: You have released me, mortal, name your
wish!
Your ten-year-old self spreads his arms wide in the manner of a
  goalkeeper.
He is guarding the fireplace for all he is worth!

You hear the wind slumping up and down the chimney.

Your ten-year-old self asks: Want to play!?
#Smirch bats his eyelashes: I just wish you would wave your wand in my
direction
>examine boy
His face is blurred.
Your ten-year-old self kicks the ball hard.

You notice the ball growing larger and larger.

You are hit full on the face!
#Beesmoke waves her cigar at Smirch and cries 'Serpenzia!' A serpent

springs out of the cigar and bites Smirch in the eye.
You feel a stinging sensation.
Your ten-year-old self falls over laughing.
>smile
What fine white teeth you have!
#Oompah pouts: How come no one ever waves a wand at me?
You notice the circle growing larger and larger.
>head ball
You head the ball back to the boy!
The boy cheers delightedly with dark arms raised!
#Beesmoke waves her cigar at Oompah and cries '£$?@&*!' The cigar looks confused and makes a camel
The ball cracks off the base of the fireplace and swerves awkwardly towards the sea-wall.
Your ten-year-old self cries: 'Watch out – it will go in the sea!'

Your ten-year-old self chases the circle with slow stringy steps.

The circle rolls to the sea-wall and disappears.

You hear the wind slumping up and down the chimney.

>west
You stand on the sea-wall. A ruined house to the east, a broken-down barn to the north. As the tide withdraws beneath you, the islands around the bay fan out in search of darkness. The grass runs in tight muscular waves towards the sea-wall's boundary.
  Obvious directions: north, east, down
  Your ten-year-old self is here
#Oompah: I need a more glamorous life
Your ten-year-old self turns his blurred face towards you
The top of the sun grazes the horizon.
>down
You climb down the sea-wall and stand up to your shins in the sea. As seaweed corkscrews under the surface, a crisp layer of water flows across the shore-stones, goosepimpling your skin.
  The only obvious exit is up.
A little ball is here (floating on the surface)
Your ten-year-old self climbs down.
#Oompah: I want to wear fancy dresses

\>get ball
As you reach for the ball it slips away west.
#Beesmoke: Well, I want to fight crime with a SUPERPOWERED CAR but I CAN'T
\>swim west
You throw yourself into the water.

As you swim out into the bay, the islands move like sharks' fins behind one another.

Your ten-year-old self swims in
The sun bobs beneath the horizon

Your ten-year-old self is dragged west by the treacherous current!

#Oompah: Maybe I should become a goth!
\>swim west
The water squirrels into your mouth, forcing you to fight for air. Your ten-year-old self is here (drowning)
Very far away and to the west, Armageddon shouts: REBOOT IN 10 MINUTES
A little ball floats in
#Cuckoospell acks
Your ten-year-old self is pulled beneath the waves!
#Sulphur acks
\>get ball
You grab the ball
#Fanboy acks
#Tundrapanic breaks out in spots
You sink.
#Uberscram runs around the room weeping: omg omg omg omg omg omg

eyestung

shield frond
soft orcrind
of the underweave

murk shot
luminous jism

44

an octopus weaselling creamily upwards

        into a lozenge of sealight

as dizzily through

           inelegant angles

of fine arterial drizzle

a jellyfish passes

#Chimneybeard freezes over
#Njar blocks all thought of the reboot by covering his ears and humming
wildly
#Draadloos hurls at the heavens
#Oompah: I like bright colours and spray tans too much though
>up
You sink

        undulating elliptically

       you scroll
  against illuminating spins

       the rich stretching of pebbles

for miles underwater
      roughly evolves
      to where you ooze

           an oil-slick
or suchlike
     of vertical loss

    the illusion of depth in the scales of fish

#Awf sings a high valedictory note, breaking all the glass in Middle Earth
As your lungs give out
       in a maze of face-reflecting bubbles

you are held fast and deep in the right hand of the sea
                    (in truth, you always have been)
#Craw spreads his tentacles: Ready for the RAPTURE!

your ten-year-old self is held deep in the left hand of the sea
                    (in truth, he always will be)

#Gruff forms a soft green ball and shyly rolls away
and the sea brings its hands together.

As the hands of the sea begin to grind
                    all your backward glances away,
your face is pressed into your ten-year-old self like a dark window-
    pane
and the sea drags you down

to a small point on the sea-floor –

the tiniest pebble to still have its lights on –

and you hear a voice say:
                    'Are you all in … is everyone in yet?'

Father reaches through the window to pull you inside –
the hair on his forearm flowing in one direction –
Smirch shouts: Goodbye not-so-cruel world!

because it is not the kind of thing you bring to a sudden end

                    making your mother westward again

*#Swain looks down from his surfboard to see the clouds of Middle Earth
    grow small*
                                as the octopus-shadows

blow east
                    across the sea-floor …

#Zigzag opens his wardrobe and steps into the night
as Father uncorks a turf-spell

46

on the dark side of the fire,

and brings
a carving-knife, a sharpened knife, a shadow-knife,

into salmon again

and Aunt Kate resumes her song:
'Are you sitting down? You're all to sit. Will everyone sit?'

#Girouette: time for breakfast anyway
>sit
You sit down

as Father lays down his knife to ask, 'In the heel
of the hunt
would a half-slice do?'

#Doodelsack: breakfast? on the east coast it's like 3 a.m. ...

and Mother turns to ask: Would you like a drink at all?
rooting in the cupboard
for the long night ahead

>nod
You nod solemnly
#Girouette: it's like 9 a.m. on the west coast
Very far away and to the east, Armageddon shouts: SERVER
SHUTTING DOWN IN 5 MINUTES

and Aunt Kate, in pursuit of St Dominic,

retrieves a locket
from her blouse

crying, 'St Anthony must have found him!'

#Doodelsack: don't you mean P.M. not A.M.?

because it is not the kind of thing you bring to a sudden end making your mother westward again

#Chimneybeard frowns: 'reboot'? what is this ' reboot' of which you
  speak? I still have to vanquish the east
#Girouette: so which west coast did you think I was on ...?
#Momworship shouts: At last! The REAL orgy can begin!

as the foam and ectoplasm

of squid-battle leaves

a school of mackerel blinded

#SirAlf fades from his chair so that all that remains is his goatee.
#Girouette: wanna party after boot?
#Awf blows out the candles and waits.

as the evolving freckles ramify

on a half-
        soft ball

              rolling

        across the
    sea-floor

#Sulphur: leaving Destructor and potions at guild. 'night everyone.

and, as Father coughs politely
              – 'Would anyone care to say grace?' –
#Doodelsack: sure if ... u know

Aunt Kate casts you an anxious glance,
            and Mother moves
through columns of sea-light

        embryo islands of chameleon green

#Doodelsack lifts his poleaxe, winking at Girouette

to pour a dark-red liquid
        well beyond what you wished –

#Girouette: sure if … I know

and, as Father looks at you again –
        'Perhaps the young master would be upstanding?' –
#Girouette lifts his long shield, winking at Doodelsack

a dark-red liquid folds
        in the direction of your glass,

and Mother says, 'Tell me when.'

A Note on Multi-User Dimensions

The long poem adopts the form of a Multi-User Dimension (or MUD), a text-based game which is played over the Internet. The poem is supposed to read like the printout of a session, or sessions, generated by one person playing a fictional MUD.

MUDs represent a small, venerable, and perhaps dying, subculture within the online gaming community. While many online multiplayer games use graphics, some, like this fictional MUD, are text-based only. The basic structure of the text, as of the game, is one of command (what the player types in, e.g. '>go west') followed by response (what the player reads as a result of their command, e.g. 'You enter a cheery glade full of elves').

MUDs are fictional worlds to which users (real people) log on. There may be hundreds of such users at any one time. These users, who often choose colourful names for their characters interact in many ways (e.g. kill, help, cheat, teach, trade, harangue). Unlike chat-rooms, MUDs are usually made up of different areas (rooms) which cumulatively amount to a world. Each room will have its own parcel of computer code. Players in the same room can usually 'see' or 'hear' each other. Players in different rooms usually cannot. Important exceptions occur where the characters use a chatline within the game, one that is associated with one or another gang or subgroup, or where a player uses the 'shout' command (a 'shout' can be read by everyone logged in to the game). In the case of my poem, these exceptions are represented by italics.

As with most computer games, death on a MUD is not 'the end' of a user's life. Normally, after death, the user's character 'resets', with some loss to their total score or to their abilities.

The fictional world of the MUD consists of human players and non-human characters. The characters, like the players, often say things and show feelings. Some times it can be hard to tell players and characters apart.

MUDs are usually themed. One can find Outer Space MUDs, Cyberpunk MUDS, Stone Age MUDs and Fantasy MUDs. The fictional MUD of the poem has a Dungeons and Dragons theme.

MUDs attract special kinds of language use. One example is the so-called 'emote'. An emote occurs when a player demonstrates an emotion theatrically rather than merely reporting it. So, for example, a player who is feeling chirpy might type 'bounce'. The other players in the same room will then read 'John bounces around' instead of 'John says: I am excited'. The text is relatively faithful to this convention.

In terms of playing-time, MUDs are quite open-ended. Users may be logged on for many hours at a time. A MUD might 'reset' or 'reboot' approximately once a day.

Those playing a MUD may approach the game with radically different purposes in mind. Some may try to accumulate more points (money, kills) than everyone else. Some may want to role-play. Some may want to explore as much of the game environment as possible. Some may want to solve a particular quest or mission within the game. Some may wish to chat with other players about politics or the weather. Some may wish to be 'alone'.

A Few MUD Terms

align: short for 'alignment'. According to their actions, players become aligned with good or evil, which in turn affects their powers and abilities.

alt: short for 'alternative character'. Players often have several characters – though they are not supposed to play more than one at a time.

basher: in a 'party', a player with an offensive emphasis.

mortal: players who accumulate sufficient points may become wizards, that is, administrators and coders of the game. Until they do, they remain mortal.

omg: oh my God.

party: short for 'war-party', and often used as a verb. A party will consist of a 'tank' and at least one 'basher'.

reboot: when the whole MUD resets. This occurs periodically e.g. every 25 hours.

tank: in a 'party', a player with a defensive emphasis.

unique: used as a noun, short for 'unique item'.

xroads: crossroads.